I0436564

TIKTOK MARKETING SIMPLIFIED

"Mastering Social Media Success: A Comprehensive Guide to Streamlining Your Brand's Growth Through TikTok Marketing"

VINCENT SIMS

Copyright ©

Dedication

"To the creators and innovators who turn seconds into trends, and to the businesses ready to captivate the world one TikTok at a time – may this book simplify your path to marketing mastery on the hottest social stage. Your creativity fuels the digital revolution."

Table of Contents

Acknowledgments

I extend my sincere gratitude to the dynamic world of TikTok for being an endless source of inspiration and innovation in the realm of digital marketing.

Special thanks to the incredible community of TikTok creators whose creativity and authenticity continue to reshape the landscape of social media.

I want to express my appreciation to everyone, whose expertise in TikTok marketing has been an invaluable guide throughout the creation of this book.

My heartfelt thanks go to the dedicated team, whose commitment to excellence has enriched the content within these pages.

I extend my appreciation to the beta readers and reviewers for their invaluable feedback and thoughtful contributions.

A special acknowledgment to the influencers and marketers on TikTok who exemplify the power of storytelling and engagement.

I am grateful for the support of my family, whose encouragement and understanding have been a constant pillar during the writing process.

Thanks to my Mentors for their insightful advice and mentorship, which significantly shaped the direction of this book.

I want to express my gratitude to the Publishing team for their collaboration and commitment to bringing this book to life.

Finally, a heartfelt thank you to the readers – your curiosity and passion for TikTok marketing drive the heartbeat of this book.

"I extend my heartfelt gratitude to the vibrant TikTok community, whose boundless creativity inspires this guide. Special thanks to the marketers, influencers, and trendsetters pushing the boundaries. To my team and mentors, your support has been invaluable. This book is a collective effort aimed at simplifying TikTok marketing for all."

Preface

"In an era where attention spans are fleeting and trends evolve in mere moments, TikTok has emerged as a powerhouse of cultural expression and marketing potential. 'TikTok Marketing Simplified' is more than a guide; it's a journey into the heart of social media innovation. Whether you're a seasoned marketer or a budding creator, this book demystifies the art of TikTok marketing, offering practical insights, strategies, and real-world examples. Prepare to unlock the full potential of your brand on the world's most dynamic stage."

Chapter 1.

Introduction to TikTok Marketing

- Understanding the TikTok Landscape

In the vast realm of social media, TikTok has swiftly risen as a dynamic platform that transcends traditional content creation. With its short-form videos and engaging features, TikTok has captured the attention of millions, making it a goldmine for marketers seeking to connect with diverse audiences. This introduction delves into understanding the TikTok landscape, shedding light on its unique characteristics and the opportunities it presents for effective marketing strategies.

The Pulse of TikTok:

TikTok's heartbeat lies in its vibrant and rapidly evolving content ecosystem. Users, known as TikTokers, showcase their creativity through short videos, often accompanied by catchy music or trending challenges. This dynamic content flow sets TikTok apart, creating a space where trends emerge swiftly, and viral moments are born in an instant. To navigate TikTok marketing successfully, one must grasp the pulse of this ever-changing landscape.

Demographic Diversity:

TikTok's user base is incredibly diverse, spanning various age groups, cultures, and interests. Understanding this broad demographic spectrum is essential for marketers aiming to tailor their content to resonate with specific audiences. Whether it's teenagers expressing themselves through dance challenges or professionals sharing industry insights, TikTok accommodates a wide array of interests, making it a versatile platform for marketing endeavors.

Short-Form Brilliance:

The essence of TikTok lies in brevity. With videos limited to a few seconds or minutes, creators are challenged to capture attention swiftly. This short-form brilliance encourages concise, impactful storytelling and demands creativity in conveying messages effectively. For marketers, this means crafting content that grabs attention instantly, resonates with the audience, and leaves a lasting impression—all within a brief time frame.

Trends and Challenges:

TikTok is synonymous with trends and challenges that spread like wildfire across the platform. Marketers can leverage these trends to align their content with popular themes, engaging the audience in a way that feels current and relevant. Staying attuned to trending challenges allows brands to participate in the collective creativity of the TikTok community, fostering a sense of connection and shared experiences.

Innovative Features:

TikTok's innovative features, such as duets, stitches, and interactive elements, provide unique opportunities for engagement. Marketers can incorporate these features into their strategies to encourage user participation, collaboration, and user-generated content. Understanding how to leverage these tools can enhance the overall impact of a TikTok marketing campaign.

As we embark on this exploration of TikTok marketing, remember that success on this platform stems from a combination of creativity, adaptability, and a genuine understanding of the community. The following chapters will delve deeper into crafting effective TikTok marketing strategies, harnessing the power of trends, and building authentic connections in the dynamic world of TikTok.

- Why TikTok for Marketing?

TikTok has rapidly become a powerhouse in the world of social media, and for marketers, its allure lies in a unique combination of factors that set it apart from other platforms. Here's a closer look at why TikTok has emerged as a compelling choice for brands and businesses looking to amplify their marketing efforts.

1. Unparalleled Reach and Engagement: TikTok boasts over a billion monthly active users globally, making it one of the most widely used social media platforms. What sets TikTok apart is its ability to capture and sustain user attention through short, engaging videos. The platform's algorithm prioritizes content

based on user preferences, ensuring that each user's feed is tailored to their interests, leading to higher engagement rates.

2. Diverse Demographics:

Unlike some platforms that cater to specific age groups, TikTok has a remarkably diverse user base. From teenagers to young adults, professionals, parents, and even seniors – TikTok attracts users of all ages and backgrounds. This diversity presents an opportunity for marketers to reach a broad audience and tailor their content to different demographics.

3. Virality and Trend Culture:

TikTok is synonymous with trends, challenges, and viral content. The platform's unique algorithm amplifies content that gains traction quickly, leading to the rapid spread of trends. Marketers can tap into this trending culture to amplify their brand message, engage with users, and potentially go viral, gaining widespread visibility in a short period.

4. Authenticity and Creativity:
TikTok thrives on authenticity and creativity. Users are drawn to content that feels genuine and showcase the creator's personality. For marketers, this presents an opportunity to humanize their brand, tell compelling stories, and connect with the audience on a more personal level. Authenticity is a currency on TikTok, and brands that embrace this ethos often find success.

5. Short-Form Content Dominance:
In an era where attention spans are shrinking, TikTok's emphasis on

short-form content aligns perfectly with the preferences of modern audiences. Marketers can deliver impactful messages within a few seconds, ensuring that their content is consumed without overwhelming the viewer. This format encourages creativity and succinct storytelling, making it ideal for capturing and retaining attention.

6. Interactive Features:
TikTok's interactive features, such as duets, stitches, and challenges, elevate user engagement to new heights. Marketers can leverage these features to encourage participation, collaboration, and user-generated content, fostering a sense of community around their brand.

In essence, TikTok's explosive growth and innovative approach to content make it a playground for marketers seeking to connect with audiences in meaningful and memorable ways. The platform's ability to facilitate creativity, drive engagement, and embrace diverse demographics positions it as a potent tool in the modern marketing arsenal. As we delve deeper into TikTok marketing strategies, understanding these unique qualities will guide us in crafting campaigns that resonate and leave a lasting impact.

- Key Trends and Statistics

Keeping a pulse on the ever-evolving landscape of TikTok is essential for marketers aiming to harness the platform's full potential. Here are some key trends and statistics that illuminate the dynamic nature of TikTok marketing:

1. Global User Base:

TikTok boasts a massive global user base, surpassing one billion monthly active users. This widespread adoption signifies the platform's universal appeal, providing marketers with an unparalleled opportunity to reach diverse audiences worldwide.

2. Age Demographics:

While TikTok initially gained popularity among younger demographics, its user base has expanded across age groups. Recent statistics reveal a significant increase in users aged 30 and above, making TikTok a platform with broad age inclusivity.

3. Short-Form Content Dominance:

Short-form videos continue to dominate TikTok's content landscape. The majority of successful content on the platform is concise and impactful, often ranging from 15 to 60 seconds. This trend emphasizes the importance of brevity and creativity in capturing the audience's attention.

4. Influencer Collaboration:
Collaborations with influencers remain a powerful strategy on TikTok. Brands leverage influencers' established follower bases to amplify their reach and credibility. TikTok influencers often play a pivotal role in driving trends and shaping the platform's cultural landscape.

5. User Engagement Metrics:
TikTok's algorithm prioritizes content based on user engagement. Metrics such as likes, comments, shares, and time spent viewing videos contribute to a video's visibility. Understanding and optimizing for these engagement factors

are crucial for marketers aiming to maximize their content's reach.

6. Hashtag Challenges:
Hashtag challenges continue to be a driving force on TikTok. Brands create and participate in challenges to encourage user-generated content and foster community engagement. Successful challenges often result in a surge of user participation, showcasing the effectiveness of this trend.

7. E-commerce Integration:
TikTok has expanded its capabilities to include e-commerce features. With functionalities like in-app shopping and product links, the platform facilitates a seamless transition from content discovery to purchase. This integration opens up new avenues for brands to drive sales directly through TikTok.

8. Authenticity and Storytelling:
Authenticity remains a cornerstone of successful TikTok marketing. Users resonate with content that feels genuine and relatable. Brands that prioritize authentic storytelling and humanize their message tend to build stronger connections with their audience.

9. Live Streaming Growth:
Live streaming has gained popularity on TikTok, providing brands with a real-time, interactive way to engage with their audience. Live sessions enable direct communication, fostering a sense of immediacy and community involvement.

10. Cultural Sensitivity:
TikTok users appreciate content that is culturally sensitive and inclusive. Brands that demonstrate an understanding of

diverse perspectives and cultural nuances tend to receive positive responses from the community.

Staying abreast of these key trends and statistics is paramount for marketers looking to navigate the ever-changing landscape of TikTok successfully. By aligning strategies with the platform's dynamics, brands can leverage these insights to create compelling, relevant content and build lasting connections with their audience.

Chapter 2.

Creating a Winning TikTok Strategy

- Defining Your Target Audience

Creating a successful TikTok strategy begins with a clear understanding of your target audience. Identify the age group, interests, and preferences of your potential viewers. Conduct research to pinpoint trends that appeal to your audience, allowing you to tailor content that aligns with their expectations. By defining your target audience, you can craft engaging and relevant TikTok content that captures attention and builds a loyal following.

- Setting Clear Marketing Objectives

When setting clear TikTok marketing objectives, start by defining specific goals tailored to the platform's dynamics. Whether it's growing your follower base, increasing video views, or driving user engagement, make your objectives measurable and aligned with your overall marketing strategy. Leverage TikTok's features such as challenges, duets, and trends to enhance brand visibility. Regularly analyze performance metrics like views, likes, and shares to gauge success and adapt your objectives as needed. Clear and targeted TikTok marketing objectives lay the foundation for a successful and impactful presence on the platform.

- Crafting Compelling Content Ideas

Crafting compelling TikTok content ideas requires a blend of creativity and awareness of platform trends. Consider leveraging popular challenges or trends relevant to your brand. Create engaging and visually appealing videos that quickly capture attention in the first few seconds. Incorporate music effectively, as sound is integral to TikTok's appeal. Experiment with different formats like tutorials, behind-the-scenes glimpses, or user-generated content to keep your audience intrigued. Remember, authenticity resonates well on TikTok, so let your brand's personality shine through your content. By staying innovative and attuned to TikTok culture, you can generate content that captivates and resonates with your audience.

Chapter 3.

Mastering TikTok's Features

- Leveraging Hashtags and Challenges

Mastering TikTok's features involves strategic use of hashtags and challenges. Utilize popular and relevant hashtags to increase the discoverability of your content. Research trending hashtags within your niche and incorporate them thoughtfully into your captions. Engaging in challenges is another powerful tool – participate in existing ones or create your own to encourage user participation. Leveraging these features not only boosts visibility but also fosters community engagement. Stay current with trending challenges and adapt them creatively to align with your brand, ensuring a dynamic and impactful presence on TikTok.

- Exploring Duets and Stitch Features

Exploring TikTok's Duets and Stitch features can elevate your content and enhance engagement. With Duets, collaborate with other users by creating split-screen videos, fostering interaction and creativity. This feature is ideal for duetting with influencers or responding to trends.

Stitch, on the other hand, allows you to incorporate snippets of others' content into your own, providing a unique way to interact with and build upon existing videos. This feature can be a powerful storytelling tool or a means to add your perspective to popular trends.

By incorporating Duets and Stitch into your TikTok strategy, you open up new avenues for collaboration, creativity, and community engagement, enriching your overall content experience on the platform.

- Understanding TikTok Analytics

Understanding TikTok analytics is pivotal for refining your content strategy. Dive into metrics such as views, likes, shares, and comments to gauge performance. Identify your most engaging content and analyze audience demographics to tailor future posts. Pay attention to the TikTok algorithm's preferences, recognizing patterns that boost visibility.

Track follower growth, and click-through rates, and watch time to measure audience retention. Utilize TikTok Pro accounts to access in-depth analytics and gain insights into when your audience is most active.

By comprehending TikTok analytics, you empower your strategy with data-driven decisions, ensuring continuous improvement and audience connection on the platform.

Chapter 4.

Building Your Brand on TikTok

- Establishing a Consistent Brand Identity

Establishing a consistent brand identity is crucial for creating a memorable and recognizable presence. Start by defining key elements such as your brand colors, logo, and tone of voice. Maintain a cohesive aesthetic across your TikTok content, aligning visuals and messaging with your brand guidelines.

Craft a consistent posting schedule to keep your audience engaged and build anticipation. Whether it's through storytelling, visual style, or specific content themes, ensure that every TikTok video reflects your brand personality.

By presenting a unified and recognizable image, you not only strengthen brand recall but also foster trust and loyalty among your TikTok audience. Consistency is key to building a lasting and impactful brand identity on the platform.

- Collaborating with Influencers

Collaborating with influencers on TikTok can significantly amplify your brand's reach and credibility. Identify influencers whose audience aligns with your target demographic, ensuring a natural fit for your brand. Reach out with a personalized and mutually beneficial proposal.

Encourage influencers to showcase your product or service authentically, leveraging their unique style. Consider participating in challenges or trends together to maximize engagement. Track performance metrics and gather feedback for future collaborations.

Influencer partnerships not only introduce your brand to a wider audience but also bring authenticity and trust, making it a powerful strategy for TikTok's marketing success.

- Engaging with the TikTok Community

Engaging with the TikTok community is essential for building a strong and loyal audience. Actively respond to comments on your videos, fostering a sense of connection with your followers. Participate in popular challenges and trends, showcasing your brand's personality in a relatable way.

Encourage user-generated content by creating challenges or asking for feedback. Share behind-the-scenes glimpses to humanize your brand. Collaborate with other creators through duets or stitches, promoting a sense of community.

By actively participating and interacting with the TikTok community, you not only increase visibility but also cultivate a genuine and enthusiastic following, enhancing the overall impact of your brand on the platform.

Chapter 5.

TikTok Advertising Essentials

- Overview of TikTok Ad Formats

TikTok advertising offers diverse formats to captivate your audience. In-feed ads seamlessly blend into users' "For You" feed, engaging them with full-screen, captivating content. Branded Hashtag Challenges encourage user participation, promoting your brand organically.

TopView Ads ensure prime visibility by appearing when users open the app, providing an immediate brand impression. Branded Effects elevate engagement by integrating your branded effects into TikTok's video creation tools.

These ad formats offer dynamic ways to connect with your target audience, making TikTok advertising a versatile and impactful tool for brand promotion and engagement. Understanding each format's strengths allows you to tailor your approach and maximize the impact of your TikTok advertising strategy.

- Setting Up Effective Ad Campaigns

Setting up effective ad campaigns on TikTok requires careful planning and strategic execution. Begin by defining clear campaign objectives—whether it's increasing brand awareness, driving traffic, or boosting sales.

Identify your target audience and tailor your ad content to resonate with their interests and preferences. Leverage TikTok's precise targeting options to reach the right users.

Choose the most suitable ad format for your goals, whether it's In-Feed Ads, Branded Hashtag Challenges, or other options. Craft compelling visuals, and engaging captions, and incorporate trending sounds to enhance your ad's appeal.

Monitor and analyze campaign performance using TikTok's analytics tools, allowing you to make data-driven adjustments for ongoing optimization.

By following these steps, you can establish and execute effective TikTok ad campaigns that resonate with your audience and achieve your marketing objectives.

- Budgeting and Monitoring Performance

Budgeting and monitoring performance are crucial aspects of a successful TikTok ad campaign. Begin by setting a clear budget that aligns with your campaign objectives. Consider allocating funds across different ad formats to diversify your reach.

Regularly monitor key performance indicators (KPIs) such as impressions, click-through rates, and engagement metrics. Use TikTok's analytics tools to gain insights into audience demographics, helping you refine your targeting strategy.

Adjust your budget allocation based on the performance of different ad sets, optimizing for the best results. Experiment with creative variations and adapt your strategy based on the real-time feedback from your campaign.

By maintaining a vigilant eye on your budget and performance metrics, you ensure that your TikTok ad campaign remains effective, efficient, and responsive to the evolving dynamics of the platform.

Chapter 6.

Measuring Success and Continuous Improvement

- Analyzing Metrics for Success

Measuring success on TikTok involves a thorough analysis of key metrics to gauge the effectiveness of your efforts. Track metrics such as views, engagement rates, shares, and click-through rates to understand how your content resonates with the audience.

Evaluate the performance of specific campaigns, hashtags, or content themes to identify what works best for your brand. Pay attention to audience demographics and geographic insights provided by TikTok analytics, helping you tailor content to your target audience.

By regularly analyzing these metrics, you can make informed decisions, refine your content strategy, and ensure ongoing improvement. Continuous monitoring and adaptation based on these insights are essential for maintaining a successful and impactful presence on TikTok.

- Adapting Strategies Based on Insights

Adapting strategies based on insights is paramount for sustained success on TikTok. Regularly review analytics to understand what resonates with your audience. Identify top-performing content, noting engagement patterns, and refine your approach accordingly.

Stay agile in responding to trends and shifts in user behavior. If certain content formats or themes prove more effective, incorporate them into your strategy. Likewise, be willing to pivot away from strategies that aren't yielding the desired results.

Flexibility is key – whether adjusting ad creative, targeting parameters, or posting times. By staying attuned to TikTok analytics and being adaptive, you ensure that your strategies remain dynamic and effective in meeting the evolving expectations of your audience.

- Future Trends in TikTok Marketing

Anticipating future trends in TikTok marketing is essential for staying ahead in the dynamic landscape of social media. Short-form video content will continue to dominate, but emerging trends may include increased use of augmented reality (AR) effects and interactive features, providing more immersive brand experiences.

Collaborations between brands and TikTok creators are likely to evolve, with a focus on authentic and creative partnerships. TikTok's algorithm may become even more refined, emphasizing personalized content tailored to individual user preferences.

As the platform evolves, keeping an eye on emerging trends, experimenting with new features, and maintaining a flexible approach will be key for brands looking to harness the full potential of TikTok marketing in the future.

www.ingramcontent.com/pod-product-compliance
Lightning Source LLC
Chambersburg PA
CBHW071217290526
45796CB00008B/272